Dominoes

Macbeth

OXFORD
UNIVERSITY PRESS

OXFORD
UNIVERSITY PRESS

Great Clarendon Street, Oxford OX2 6DP

Oxford University Press is a department of the University of Oxford.
It furthers the University's objective of excellence in research, scholarship,
and education by publishing worldwide in

Oxford New York

Auckland Bangkok Buenos Aires Cape Town Chennai
Dar es Salaam Delhi Hong Kong Istanbul Karachi Kolkata
Kuala Lumpur Madrid Melbourne Mexico City Mumbai
Nairobi São Paulo Shanghai Taipei Tokyo Toronto

OXFORD and OXFORD ENGLISH are registered trade marks of
Oxford University Press in the UK and in certain other countries

ISBN-13: 978 0 19 424453 4
ISBN-10: 0 19 424453 9

A complete recording of this Dominoes edition of *Macbeth*
is available on cassette ISBN 0 19 424446 6

Printed in Hong Kong

ACKNOWLEDGEMENTS

The publisher would like to thank the following for kind permission to reproduce photographs:

Alamy Images pp6 (tent/Profimedia.CZ s.r.o.), 6 (witch/SuperStock), 12 (bells/PCL), 25
(pot/David Crausby), 25 (dining hall/Angel Terry); Aquarius Library p39 (Romeo and
Juliet/T.C.F); bfi Stills, Posters & Designs ppivcd (Banquo & son/British Film Institute), 14
(mountains/), 19 (horses/); Corbis ppive (Queen Elizabeth I/Fine Art Photographic Library),
ivf (James VI/John de Critz/Fine Art Photographic Library), 6 (soldier/Rob Howard), 25
(ghost/Reuters), 25 (apples/Becky Luigart-Stayner), 25 (hut/Richard Cummins); Hemera
pp18 (crown), 24 (dagger), 31 (cauldron); Kobal Collection pp7 (castle/Columbia), 9
(Macbeth/Columbia), 26 (witches/Columbia); PunchStock pp6 (Liberty Bell/Photodisc), 6
(vials of blood/Comstock), 6 (wine bottle & glass/Stockbyte), 25 (fireplace/Thinkstock); Rex
Features pp39 (Mel Gibson/Miramax/Everett), 39 (Eric Porter/Reg Wilson); Ronald Grant
Archive ppivb (Lady Macbeth 1971), iva (Jon Finch & Francesca Annis), 1 (scene from 1971
Macbeth/Columbia), 4 (Jon Finch & Francesca Annis), 15 (Banquo & Macbeth/Columbia
Pictures), 20 (Macbeth & Lady Macbeth/Caliban Films/Playboy Productions), 22 (Macbeth &
Lady Macbeth), 33 (Macbeth), 36 (fighting/Columbia Pictures)

Project page illustrations by Ben Hasler/NB Illustration

Dominoes

SERIES EDITORS: BILL BOWLER AND SUE PARMINTER

Macbeth

WILLIAM SHAKESPEARE

Text adaptation by Alistair McCallum

LEVEL ONE ■ 400 HEADWORDS

William Shakespeare (1564–1616) was born and grew up in Stratford-upon-Avon. At the age of twenty-five, he left his wife and children in Stratford, moved to London, and started working as an actor and writer at the Globe Theatre. Shakespeare wrote more than thirty plays, and some fine poetry, too. He wrote *Macbeth* in about 1606 and he perhaps wrote a play about Scotland because the Scottish King James was the new King of England at this time and he came from the family of Banquo in this story. Shakespeare's plays are still famous all over the world today, and for many people he is the greatest writer in English. Another Shakespeare story, *The Tempest*, is also available as a Domino.

OXFORD
UNIVERSITY PRESS

BEFORE READING

1 Here are some of the people in the story of Macbeth. Who is good and who is bad, do you think? Write **G** (good) or **B** (bad).

a Macbeth, a soldier **b** Lady Macbeth, Macbeth's wife **c** Banquo, Macbeth's friend **d** Fleance, Banquo's son

2 At the end of the story, only one of these people is alive. Who?

3 Match the information about the King and Queen of England in Shakespeare's time.

Elizabeth I   James I

a . . . .'s parents were Henry VIII and Anne Boleyn.

b . . . . was King from 1603 to 1625.

c . . . . wasn't married.

d . . . . was Queen from 1559 to 1603.

e . . . . had three sons and five daughters.

f . . . . was very popular in England.

g . . . . was from Scotland.

Chapter 1 ✠ Soldier, general, king

It was a cold, dark, rainy day in Scotland a thousand years ago. Three **witches** waited.

'What is going to happen, sisters?'

'We are going to meet someone.'

'Who are we going to meet, sisters?'

'Macbeth.'

'When are we going to meet him?'

'After the **battle**.'

✠

'Who can help us?' said Duncan, **King** of Scotland. 'The King of Norway wants to take our country. His **soldiers** are here, and they're killing my men.'

Duncan waited for many hours in his **camp** to hear about the battle. Things were very bad. Duncan was afraid.

Suddenly a Scottish soldier ran into the camp and came in front of the king. He was tired and dirty from the battle, and there was **blood** on his face. 'My **lord**,' he cried. 'The Norwegian **general** is dead! The Norwegian soldiers are running away! Scotland is free once again.'

witch a woman who can fly through the sky and do bad things

battle when soldiers from different countries fight

king the most important man in a country

soldier a person who fights for his or her country

camp a place where soldiers stay for a short time

blood this is red; you see it when you cut your hand

lord an important man from a good family

general a very important man in an army

The Norwegian general is dead!

'That's wonderful,' said King Duncan. 'Who killed their general?'

'His name is Macbeth, and he's the best soldier in Scotland.'

⁂

Macbeth was tired. He walked slowly to King Duncan's camp with his friend Banquo.

'What a long battle!' said Macbeth.

'A lot of our friends are dead,' said Banquo, 'but the Norwegian soldiers are going home. And they're never coming back!'

Suddenly they saw the three witches in front of them.

'Who are you? What are you doing?' asked Banquo.

They didn't speak to him, but they looked at Macbeth.

'Macbeth!' cried the witches.

'What!? How do you know my name?' he asked.

They spoke again, all at the same time: 'Macbeth, the soldier! Macbeth, the general! Macbeth, the king!'

'General? King? What are these women talking about?' Macbeth asked Banquo. 'I'm a soldier – nothing more!'

'Is this true?' Banquo asked them. 'Can you see into the **future**? Speak to *me*! What can you tell me?'

The witches looked at him. 'Banquo, the father of kings!'

'Who are you?' asked Macbeth. 'Tell us more!' But suddenly the witches weren't there! Macbeth and Banquo looked here and there, but they could see nobody.

'Perhaps they were witches?' said Macbeth.

Banquo laughed. 'Or perhaps we are tired after the battle and we **imagined** them,' he answered.

⁂

future what is going to happen

imagine to think

2

King Duncan was very happy when Macbeth and Banquo arrived at his camp.

'Well done, my **brave** friends! Macbeth, I want to say thank you, from everyone in Scotland. Macbeth, you are now the general of the Scottish **army**.'

Everyone was excited. 'Macbeth, the bravest man in Scotland!' they cried.

But Macbeth and Banquo stood quietly and thought about the three witches' **words**. *Macbeth the soldier! Macbeth the general! Macbeth the king!*

At Macbeth's home, his wife, **Lady** Macbeth, waited, day after day. But one day a letter arrived. It was a long letter from her husband.

After the battle, Banquo and I met three women. They were witches, and they can see into the future! 'You're going to be a general,' they told me – and they were right! Next, they said: 'Macbeth, you're going to be king!' I can't stop thinking about it!

Lady Macbeth was excited. Her husband . . . King of Scotland! 'I want to be **Queen** of Scotland,' she thought. 'The witches are right. My husband is going to be king. Nothing can stop us!' She began reading again:

King Duncan is coming to stay with us soon! His son Malcolm is coming too, and Banquo, and Macduff. We must be ready . . .

Lady Macbeth cried excitedly. 'King Duncan! In our house?

brave not afraid

army a number of soldiers

word something we say or write

lady an important woman from a good family

queen the wife of a king

Macbeth wasn't happy.

Good! He's king now, but things are going to change. Scotland is going to have a new king!'

⁂

When Macbeth came home, his wife began to talk about their future. 'We're going to be rich and happy,' she said, 'when you are king.'

But Macbeth wasn't happy. 'What are you talking about?' he cried. 'How can I be king? Scotland has a king!'

'Listen. You're a soldier, and you often kill men in battles,' said his wife. 'King Duncan is coming here tonight.'

'What are you saying?' asked Macbeth.

'You must be brave. Remember the witches: you are going to be king. Duncan must die here in our house. What's the matter? Are you afraid?'

⁂

That evening King Duncan arrived at Macbeth's house with his son Malcolm, and with Banquo.

'What a beautiful house!' said King Duncan.

'Yes, my lord, and the garden is wonderful too,' said Banquo.

It was a sunny afternoon, and the king and Banquo walked slowly past the trees and flowers to Macbeth's door.

Lady Macbeth came out of the house. 'Thank you for visiting us, my lord. We're very happy to see you.'

'Lady Macbeth!' said the king warmly. 'How are you? And where is your husband, the general? Is he well?'

Lady Macbeth smiled. 'Yes, my lord. He is waiting to meet you. Please, come in.'

'He is a brave man, you know,' said King Duncan. 'He killed many of our **enemies**. Scotland is free once more – and we must thank your husband for that!'

In the evening, everyone had dinner. They all sat at a big table – the king, Malcolm, Macbeth and his wife, Banquo, and all their friends. Everyone ate, drank **wine**, talked and laughed. But Macbeth left the room early. His wife came out to find him.

'I can't do it,' said Macbeth. 'I can't kill Duncan. He's our king, and a good man. Let's forget about it.'

'What!' cried Lady Macbeth angrily. 'Remember the witches! You are going to be king! Do you want to wait for years and years? Are you a man? Or are you afraid?'

'Of course I'm not afraid. But things can always go wrong!

'Nothing can go wrong. Listen. Duncan has two **servants**. Tonight, I'm going to give them a lot of wine. When they're sleeping, you can go into Duncan's room. You must use their knives. Do you understand?'

'Yes . . . and we can put blood on his servants' hands!' said Macbeth.

'That's right,' said Lady Macbeth. 'And what are people going to think when they find the dead king tomorrow? His servants killed him, of course, not you! Now, you see the **bell** over there; tonight, when everything is ready, I'm going to **ring** it. Be brave, my husband!'

enemy people who are not friends of your country

wine a red or white drink; when you drink a lot you feel happy and sleepy

servant a person who works for someone rich

bell a metal thing that makes a noise when you move it

ring (*past* **rang**) to make a noise with a bell

READING CHECK

What do they say?

a A Scottish soldier says to King Duncan: 　4

b The witches say to Macbeth: ☐

c Macbeth says to the witches: ☐

d Banquo says to the witches: ☐

e King Duncan says to Macbeth and Banquo: ☐

f Lady Macbeth says to King Duncan: ☐

g Macbeth says to his wife: ☐

h Lady Macbeth says to her husband: ☐

❶ Well done, my brave friends!

❷ Macbeth, the king!

❸ Speak to me! What can you tell *me*?

❹ My lord, the Norwegian general is dead!

❺ Thank you for visiting us, my lord.

❻ What!? How do you know my name?

❼ Are you a man? Or are you afraid?

❽ I can't do it.

WORD WORK

1 These words don't match the pictures. Correct them.

a ~~blood~~

. . . . camp . . . .

b wine

. . . .

c soldier

. . . .

d camp

. . . .

e bell

. . . .

f witch

. . . .

2 Use the letters to make words from Chapter 1. Then write the sentences.

a In the *eltabt*, Macbeth kills the Norwegian *raengel*.

.... In the battle, Macbeth kills the Norwegian general. ....

b Macbeth is a soldier in the Scottish *yamr*. The Norwegian soldiers are his *sineeme*.

. . . .

c 'Did we see three *sctiwhe* and hear their *drows*? Or did we *menigia* them?'

. . . .

d 'When the bell *girns*, go into *gink* Duncan's room.'

. . . .

e 'His *avrssetn* are sleeping. Be *vaber*!'

. . . .

GUESS WHAT

**What happens in the next chapter?
Tick the boxes.**

a In the night, Macbeth goes into
Duncan's room. What happens?

1 ☐ Duncan cries for help.

2 ☐ Duncan's servants wake up.

3 ☐ Macbeth kills Duncan.

b In the morning, what happens to
Duncan's servants?

1 ☐ They run away.

2 ☐ Macbeth kills them.

3 ☐ Banquo asks them a lot
of questions.

Chapter 2 ✻ Murder in the night

It was late at night. It was dark in the house, but Macbeth wasn't in bed. He was downstairs. Suddenly he heard a noise. 'Who's there?' he called.

'It's me,' answered Banquo. 'It's late, and I'm going to bed.'

'Me too,' said Macbeth.

'Do you remember those three women? They called you a general – and a king.'

'Which women? Oh, those three . . . no, I never think about them.'

'Good. It's best to forget about them. Goodnight, Macbeth.'

'Goodnight, Banquo.'

✻

It was after midnight. Everyone in the house was in bed, but downstairs Macbeth waited and waited.

'I can see something,' he thought. 'Is it a **dagger**? It's there, in front of my eyes!' He put his hand out. 'I can see it, but I can't take it in my hand! What's happening? Am I imagining things?'

Suddenly he heard a noise. It was the bell!

'No more words,' he thought. 'It's time to do it. Duncan must die!'

✻

Lady Macbeth was in her room. 'Everything is going well,' she thought. 'Duncan's servants are sleeping because they drank a lot of wine. Their daggers are on the table, so my husband can find them . . .'

Suddenly Macbeth came into the room. In his hands

dagger a knife for killing people

In his hands were the two daggers.

were the two daggers. There was blood on them.

'I can hear **voices**,' he said quietly. 'People are talking. Listen! Someone is crying "Murder!". Can you hear?'

'No, I can't. You're imagining things! There are no voices. Everyone is sleeping,' said Lady Macbeth. Then she saw the servants' daggers in Macbeth's hands.

'Why are you carrying those?' she asked angrily. 'Take them back to Duncan's room, and put them next to his servants! Why did you forget?'

Macbeth didn't move. 'I'm not going back,' he said.

voice you use this to speak

'Give them to me, then,' said his wife. 'Why are you afraid? Duncan is dead. He can't **hurt** us now!' She took the daggers and went quickly to Duncan's room.

After some time Lady Macbeth came back to her room. 'The servants have blood on their hands and faces now,' she said to her husband. 'So they are the king's killers, of course. Not us. Everyone's going to think that.'

Just then, they heard a noise. It was a loud **knock**. There was someone at the front door! Macbeth was afraid, and he couldn't move or speak. There was another knock, and another.

'Come on!' said Lady Macbeth. 'We must **wash** our hands. Our servant can go to the door.'

Macbeth's servant opened the door. The visitor was Macduff. He was a soldier, and one of Duncan's friends.

'Good morning, **sir**,' said the servant. 'Everyone is sleeping, I think. Shall I **wake** the general?'

Just then, Macbeth came downstairs.

'Macbeth! Good morning, my friend,' said Macduff. 'King Duncan wants to see me today. He asked me to call early in the morning. Is the king upstairs?'

'Yes, he is. He's sleeping, I think. Shall I go and wake him?' asked Macbeth.

'No, that's all right. Can you take me to his room?'

The two men went upstairs to the king's room, and Macduff went in.

At once Macduff came out of the room again, and his face was white. 'This is **terrible**, terrible! The king is dead! It's **murder**!'

'The king? Dead?' said Macbeth. 'No! It isn't true!'

hurt (*past* **hurt**) to make someone feel bad

knock the noise when someone hits a door

wash to make something clean

sir you say this when you talk to an important man

wake (*past* **woke**) to stop sleeping

terrible very bad

murder the time when a murderer kills someone

'Go in, and look. I cannot tell you more,' answered Macduff.

Then he began to call. 'Wake up! Get out of bed, everyone! Banquo! Malcolm! There's a murderer in the house!'

Doors opened, people came out of their rooms, and everybody began talking at the same time.

Lady Macbeth came out of her room. 'What's the matter? Why is there all this noise?' she asked.

'My lady, I have terrible **news**,' said Macduff. 'Our king – your father, Malcolm – he's dead. Someone murdered him in the night.'

'Oh, no!' cried Banquo. 'Is it true? Who killed him?'

'I don't know,' said Macduff. 'His servants, perhaps. There's blood on their hands, and on their daggers. I wanted to talk to them, but I couldn't wake them.'

Just then, Macbeth came out of Duncan's room. 'Those servants were murderers. But they're never going to hurt anyone again. I killed them!'

'Why did you do that?' asked Macduff angrily. 'Now we can't ask them any questions. How can we learn the **truth** about the king's murder now?'

'I'm sorry,' said Macbeth. 'I was angry. You must understand! Who can stop and think when a terrible murder happens? They murdered our king, our wonderful king, and so I killed them . . .'

Suddenly Lady Macbeth cried out and **fainted**.

'Carry the lady to her room,' said Banquo. 'Listen, everyone. Later this morning, when we are ready, we must all meet and talk about this terrible news. We must be careful. Scotland has new enemies!'

news when someone tells you something that is new

truth what is true

faint to fall down suddenly because you are ill, or afraid

READING CHECK

Correct six more mistakes in this summary of Chapter 2.

Banquo

Downstairs, late at night, Macbeth meets ~~Malcolm~~. They talk about the two witches.

Banquo goes to bed, and Macbeth waits downstairs. Suddenly Macbeth sees the bell —

it's time to go to King Duncan's room. Duncan's servants are sleeping because Lady

Macbeth gave them a lot of coffee. Macbeth kills the queen using the servants' daggers.

Later, Macduff comes to the house. He is one of Duncan's enemies. When he sees the

king's dead body, he calls: 'Get out of bed, everyone! There's a murderer in the house!'

After that, Banquo kills the servants. How can they learn the truth about the murder now?

WORD WORK

1 Find words in the bell to complete the sentences.

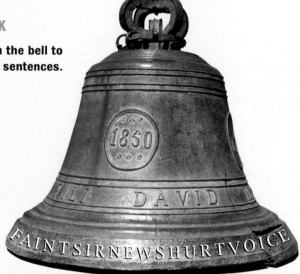

1850

DAVID

FAINTSIRNEWSHURTVOICE

a Excuse me, ..sir..... Can I see your passport?

b I can't hear the teacher. Her .... is very quiet.

c That man looks very white. He's ill. I think he's going to ....

d What happened yesterday? I didn't hear the .... on the radio this morning.

e Don't sit on the cat! You're going to .... it.

2 Find words from Chapter 2 to complete the sentences. Write the words in the crossword.

a He killed a man because he was angry. He's a m urderer.

b Macbeth kills Duncan with his servants' d _ _ _ _ _ _ .

c There's someone at the door. I heard a k _ _ _ _ on it.

d It's very cold and it's raining. The weather is t _ _ _ _ _ _ _ today

e Breakfast is ready. Can you w _ _ _ the children?

f Did you break that window? Don't tell me any stories now. Tell the t _ _ _ _!

g All my shirts are dirty. I must w _ _ _ them.

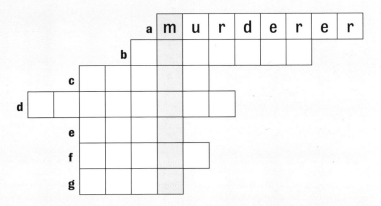

3 Who is not going to be the father of kings? Read the blue squares and write his name. _ _ _ _ _ _ _ .

GUESS WHAT

What happens in the next chapter? Tick the boxes.

a King Duncan's son Malcolm . . .

1 ☐ is the new King of Scotland.

2 ☐ kills Macbeth.

3 ☐ leaves Macbeth's house.

b Banquo thinks that . . . murdered the king.

1 ☐ Malcolm

2 ☐ Macbeth

3 ☐ Macduff

Chapter 3 ✳ A new king

The king's son, Malcolm, was **worried**. 'I must leave at once,' he thought. 'Someone murdered my father. Perhaps they're going to kill me too? I must get help – for me and for my country. Perhaps the King of England can help me. I must go and see.'

He spoke to no one, but he got on his horse and he left Macbeth's house quickly.

He left Macbeth's house quickly.

Later, all the most important people in Scotland met and talked about the terrible news.

'Who's going to be our new king?' they asked. 'What about Duncan's son, Malcolm?'

'Malcolm isn't in Scotland with us now. He ran away when his father died.'

'Then what about Macbeth? He's our best soldier, and the general of our army. Let's make him our king!'

'Yes! Macbeth!' Everyone cried excitedly. 'Macbeth, King of Scotland!'

worried not happy about something and thinking a lot about it

✳

Banquo was **alone** in a big room in Macbeth's **castle**.

'The witches were right about Macbeth,' he thought. 'He's the King now, he's rich, and he lives in the biggest castle in Scotland. But how did Duncan die? Did Macbeth murder him? Yes, he did, I think. And I'm afraid.'

Then Banquo remembered the witches' words: *Banquo, the father of kings!* Banquo thought about his son, Fleance. 'Perhaps Fleance is going to be king one day?'

Just then, Macbeth and his wife, the queen, came into the room. Many lords, ladies and servants came in with them.

'Banquo, my good friend,' said Macbeth, 'we are having a **banquet** at the castle this evening. Can you come?'

'Of course, my lord,' answered Banquo.

'Are you going to **ride** this afternoon?'

alone with nobody

castle a big old building; a rich person lives here

banquet a big, important dinner

ride to go on a horse

Are you going to ride?

'Yes, my lord.'

'Are you going far?'

'No, my lord. I'm coming back later this evening.'

'Remember the banquet.'

'Of course, my lord.'

'And are you riding alone, or with your son?'

'Fleance is coming with me, my lord,' answered Banquo. 'And we're leaving soon.'

'Good. Banquo, did you hear about Malcolm?' asked Macbeth. 'He murdered his father, King Duncan – we all know the truth now. And I have more terrible news,' Macbeth went on. 'Malcolm's in England now, and he's making **trouble**. We must talk – tomorrow, perhaps?'

Macbeth smiled at Banquo when he left, but he wasn't happy: Macbeth was worried. He too remembered the witches' words: *Banquo, the father of kings!*

'Does Banquo know the truth about Duncan's murder? And did I murder Duncan for Banquo's son to be king after me?' he cried.

✳

Later, when Macbeth was alone, a servant came into the room.

'There are two visitors here. They want to see you, my lord,' he said.

'Good. I'd like to see them now,' answered Macbeth.

The two men came in. 'I have some important work for you,' said Macbeth. 'There is a man called Banquo. He's a good man, everyone thinks, but it's not true. He is our enemy. He must die. Do you understand?'

'Yes, my lord,' said the two men. 'We're not afraid.'

trouble problems

'Good. He's riding with his son now. When they come

back this evening, you must kill them. Remember: his son must die too!'

The men left, and soon after Lady Macbeth came in.

'Why are you here, my lord, far from your friends? What are you thinking of?' she asked.

She looked at his worried face.

'All right, you killed Duncan,' she said. 'But when you can't change something, don't think about it.'

'Yes,' answered Macbeth. 'You're right. Duncan is dead – but Banquo and his son Fleance live.'

'And what can we do about that?' asked Lady Macbeth.

'Don't ask me now, my love,' smiled Macbeth. 'But wait and see.'

When Banquo and his son came back to the castle, it was dark. They got off their horses and began walking to the castle door. Suddenly two men ran out from behind some trees.

'Who are you? What do you want?' asked Banquo.

The two men didn't answer.

'Are you ready?' said one of the men. 'Let's do it! Now!'

The two men suddenly took out their daggers and **stabbed** Banquo. They were very quick, and Banquo couldn't stop them.

'They're going to kill me, Fleance, but you must stay **alive**!' he cried. 'Run, Fleance! Run!'

Fleance ran away at once. 'Quick! Let's go after him,' said one of the murderers. 'We must get him, too, or the king's going to be very angry.'

The murderers ran after Fleance, but they couldn't find him because it was dark.

stab to hit with a knife or dagger

alive living

17

READING CHECK

Put these sentences in the correct order. Number them 1–9.

a ☐ All the most important people in Scotland meet.

b ☐ Two men visit Macbeth.

c ☐ The murderers kill Banquo.

d ☐ Banquo and Fleance get off their horses and begin walking to the castle.

e ☐ Macbeth is the new King of Scotland.

f ☐1 Malcolm leaves Macbeth's house.

g ☐ The murderers run after Fleance, but they can't find him.

h ☐ Two men run out from behind some trees.

i ☐ Macbeth asks Banquo to come to his banquet.

WORD WORK

1 Find seven more words from Chapter 3 in the wordsquare.

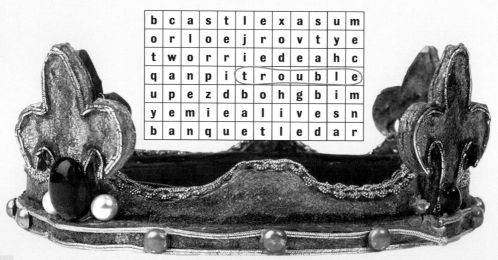

b	c	a	s	t	l	e	x	a	s	u	m
o	r	l	o	e	j	r	o	v	t	y	e
t	w	o	r	r	i	e	d	e	a	h	c
q	a	n	p	i	t	r	o	u	b	l	e
u	p	e	z	d	b	o	h	g	b	i	m
y	e	m	i	e	a	l	i	v	e	s	n
b	a	n	q	u	e	t	l	e	d	a	r

2 Use the words from Activity 1 to complete Fleance's note.

I'm in terrible a) <u>trouble</u>. Two murderers killed my
father. They b) _____ him with their daggers. We
were near Macbeth's c) _____. There's going to be
a d) _____ there tonight. I'm very e) _____ ,
because the murderers want to kill me too. My mother
is dead, and I have no brothers or sisters, so I'm
f) _____ now, and nobody can help me. I'm going
to find my horse and g) _____ far away from here.
I don't want to die. I want to stay h) _____ !

GUESS WHAT

The next chapter is called 'A ghost at the table'. What are you going to read about?

a ☐ King Duncan's ghost   b ☐ Banquo's ghost   c ☐ Fleance's ghost

Chapter 4 ✤ A ghost at the table

At the king's castle, everything was ready for the banquet. All the most important lords and ladies in Scotland were there.

'Please, come into the **dining-room** and sit down at the table, everyone,' said Lady Macbeth.

Just then, two men arrived at the castle. The queen and all the lords and ladies went into the dining-room and sat down at the table, but Macbeth waited for a short time before he went after them. He spoke quietly to the two men.

'There's blood on your face,' he said to the first man.

'It's Banquo's blood, my lord,' said the man.

'Is Banquo dead then?' asked Macbeth.

'Yes, my lord,' said the man happily. 'I killed him with my knife.'

'Good man!' said Macbeth. 'And tell me, did you kill Fleance, too?'

'No, my lord. Fleance ran away.'

dining-room the room in a house where people eat

Macbeth went into the dining room.

'Oh, no!' cried Macbeth angrily. 'Why is it all going wrong? Fleance is alive! And he must die too! But Banquo's dead, you say?'

'Yes my lord. Dead and cold.'

'Good. So, Banquo's dead but Fleance lives. Well, come back here tomorrow. We must meet again and talk more about this. It's very important!'

The two men left. Just then, Lady Macbeth came out of the dining-room. 'What's the matter, my love? Everyone is waiting for you. Come and eat with us!'

❋

Macbeth went into the dining-room. There were a lot of people in the room, and there was a lot of **food** and wine on the table.

'Where's my good friend Banquo?' asked Macbeth. 'He isn't here. He's late!'

'It doesn't matter,' said Lady Macbeth. 'Come and sit down. Your chair is here.'

Macbeth walked to the table, then he stopped suddenly. There was a **ghost** in his chair! The ghost looked up at him. It was Banquo and his face was bloody!

'What's happening?' cried Macbeth. He was afraid. The ghost looked at him, but didn't speak. 'Why are you looking at me? I didn't do it!' Macbeth cried.

Everyone at the table looked at Macbeth. 'What's wrong, my lord?' they asked. 'Why are you worried?'

They couldn't see the ghost – but Macbeth could see it.

'I'm sorry, everyone, my husband isn't well,' said Lady Macbeth.

She took Macbeth out of the room. 'What's the matter with you?' she asked angrily. 'You're imagining things

food things that you eat

ghost a dead person that a living person sees or hears

again. First it was a dagger in front of you on the night of Duncan's murder, and now this ghost. What's wrong? Don't be afraid. Be a man. Be brave. There's no one in your chair!'

'But he's a dead man. How can he come back?' said Macbeth. 'And how can you look at him and not be afraid?'

'What are you talking about? What are people going to think? There is no ghost! Your friends at the table are worried. Now, go back and sit in your chair!'

They went back into the dining-room. Macbeth couldn't see the ghost now, so he sat down happily.

'I'm sorry, my friends,' he said to his visitors. 'Sometimes I feel ill and I begin to imagine things; but please don't worry about me. I'm better now. Come on, let's have some wine! Let's drink to our friend Banquo! He isn't here with us tonight and I'm sorry for that!'

Just then, Banquo's ghost came through the door and walked across the room. Macbeth cried out again. 'Get away from me!'

'Get away from me!'

He stood up suddenly. 'You're dead. Dead and cold! There's no blood in you! And those terrible eyes! Don't look at me! Leave me alone!'

'What's the king saying?' asked the lords and ladies at the table. 'What's he looking at? Why is he afraid?'

Lady Macbeth was worried. 'Don't listen to him. I'm sorry, everyone. You must all go,' she cried. 'The king is ill. No more questions, please. He gets worse when you ask him questions. Please, go now! Don't wait. Go at once!'

※

The visitors all left, and the castle was quiet. It was very late, but Macbeth didn't go to bed. He sat and thought for a long time.

'Macduff didn't come to our banquet,' he said. 'Why not? I asked him to come. When the king speaks, everyone must listen. Is Macduff my enemy now too?'

'You look tired,' said his wife. 'You must sleep.'

'I can't sleep. I'm not happy. Everything is going wrong.'

Macbeth thought for a minute. 'I know,' he said. 'Tomorrow I'm going to find the witches. I want to ask them some questions. I must know the truth!'

※

The three witches were in a dirty old **hut**. In front of them was a big **pot** on a **fire**. They put a lot of **strange** and terrible things in the pot – an animal's head, a tooth, a dead man's hand, some blood . . .

'Someone is coming, sisters.'

Just then, Macbeth ran into the hut. 'Listen!' he said at once. 'I have some important questions, and I need answers. Do you understand? I want to know more about the future!'

hut a little house

pot you cook in this

fire this is red and hot and it burns

strange not usual

READING CHECK

1 What do they say?

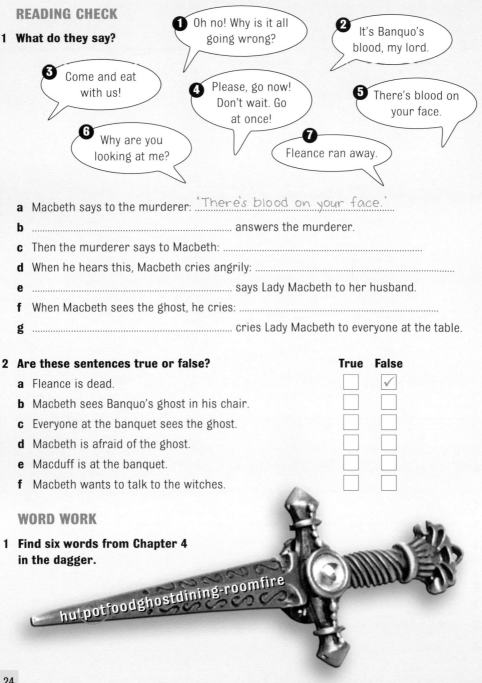

1 Oh no! Why is it all going wrong?

2 It's Banquo's blood, my lord.

3 Come and eat with us!

4 Please, go now! Don't wait. Go at once!

5 There's blood on your face.

6 Why are you looking at me?

7 Fleance ran away.

a Macbeth says to the murderer: ....'There's blood on your face.'....

b .... answers the murderer.

c Then the murderer says to Macbeth: ....

d When he hears this, Macbeth cries angrily: ....

e .... says Lady Macbeth to her husband.

f When Macbeth sees the ghost, he cries: ....

g .... cries Lady Macbeth to everyone at the table.

2 Are these sentences true or false?

	True	False
a Fleance is dead.	☐	✓
b Macbeth sees Banquo's ghost in his chair.	☐	☐
c Everyone at the banquet sees the ghost.	☐	☐
d Macbeth is afraid of the ghost.	☐	☐
e Macduff is at the banquet.	☐	☐
f Macbeth wants to talk to the witches.	☐	☐

WORD WORK

1 Find six words from Chapter 4 in the dagger.

hutpotfoodghostdining-roomfire

2 Match the words in Activity 1 with the pictures

a . . . . . . pot . . . . . .

b . . . .

c . . . .

d . . . .

e . . . .

f . . . .

GUESS WHAT

What happens in the next chapter? Tick the boxes.

a After he talks to the witches,
   Macbeth feels . . .

1 ☐ happy.

2 ☐ sad.

3 ☐ angry.

b Macduff is . . .

1 ☐ at home, with his family.

2 ☐ in England, with Malcolm.

3 ☐ dead.

c At night, Lady Macbeth...

1 ☐ can't sleep.

2 ☐ sleeps quietly.

3 ☐ walks and talks in her sleep.

Chapter 5 ✤ The witches tell Macbeth more

'Watch, and listen,' said the witches. The fire under the pot got bigger and bigger. Suddenly there was the noise of **thunder**. Then Macbeth saw something strange over the witches' pot. It was a soldier's head!

Macbeth began to speak, but the witches stopped him. 'He knows your question,' they said. 'Listen, but don't speak.'

The soldier's head looked at Macbeth and cried, 'Macbeth! Macduff is going to hurt you! Be careful!'

'I'm going to remember that,' thought Macbeth. 'Macduff must die!'

There was more thunder. The head went suddenly from in front of Macbeth's eyes, and now over the pot there was a **baby**. There was blood on its face and body, but it smiled at Macbeth.

'Be happy, Macbeth! No mother's son can hurt you!' said the baby.

'Good,' thought Macbeth. 'Everyone has a mother. I'm **safe**!'

thunder a loud noise in the sky when there is a storm

baby a very young child

safe when nothing bad can happen to you

'Watch and listen.'

Next came a young boy. There was a **crown** on his head, and he had a tree in his hand.

'Your enemies cannot hurt you, Macbeth!' he said. 'But when the trees near your castle begin to walk, there is going to be trouble!'

Macbeth laughed at this. 'Good, very good! Trees can't walk! I'm going to live safely for a long, long time!'

But Macbeth had one last question for the witches. 'When we last met, you called Banquo "the father of kings". Is this true?'

'Do not ask,' said the witches. 'Why do you want to know?'

'Tell me!' cried Macbeth angrily. Just then, a man walked across the room, and a second, and a third – and they all had crowns on their heads. They were kings of Scotland – the kings of the future – and they were Banquo's children, grandchildren, and great-grandchildren!

'No!' cried Macbeth. 'It's not true!'

After all the kings came a ghost. It was the ghost of Banquo! He looked at Macbeth and smiled.

⁜

Macbeth ran back to his castle. He was angry with the witches. 'They called Banquo the father of kings. And Fleance is alive!'

Later, one of Macbeth's **spies** came to the castle. 'My lord, I have some news about Macduff. He is in England, with Malcolm. I think they're going to make trouble for us.'

'Well, Macduff,' thought Macbeth. 'You are in England, but your wife and children are here in Scotland. You are safe – but they are not! They're going to die, all of them!'

⁜

crown a king wears this on his head

spy a person who tries to learn secret things

When Macduff arrived in England, Malcolm was happy to see him.

'Macduff, my good friend! Do you have any news from Scotland?' he asked.

'Only bad news, Malcolm. Macbeth isn't a king, he's a murderer. He killed your father, and he wants to kill all his enemies. Everyone in Scotland is afraid of him. We must stop him now, or the people of Scotland can never be happy again. We must stop him before he does worse things.'

Just then a **messenger** arrived from Scotland. He had some terrible news for Macduff.

'What is it?' asked Macduff quickly.

'Your wife, my lord. Your wife and all your children are dead!' said the man.

For a minute Macduff stood quietly and said nothing, and then suddenly he found his voice.

'What! All my family? Dead? And I wasn't there! I couldn't help them!' he cried. 'Who did this? No, wait. You don't need to tell me. I know. It was Macbeth. I'm going to kill him for this!'

'Macduff, nothing can bring back your family,' said Malcolm, 'but perhaps I can help you. Listen. The king of England is my friend. He knows about Macbeth. He's going to help us. An army of ten thousand English soldiers is ready. We're going to **attack** Macbeth's castle. Are you going to come with us?'

⁂

It was late at night. One of Lady Macbeth's servants was with the doctor. 'I'm worried about the queen,' said the servant. 'At night, when she's sleeping, she sometimes gets

messenger someone who brings news

attack to start fighting

up and walks out of her room. She talks, and does strange things.'

'When she talks in her sleep, what does she say?' asked the doctor.

'I'm sorry, sir, but I don't want to tell anyone. Look, here she comes now!'

Lady Macbeth's door opened, and she walked out. She carried a **candle** in her hand.

'Her eyes are open, but she's sleeping,' said the doctor. 'Where did she find the candle?'

'She always has a candle by her bed, sir,' said the servant. 'She's afraid of the night, and doesn't like it when it's dark.'

Lady Macbeth put down the candle and began to speak. 'We must wash our hands. Are you a man or are you afraid? No one is going to know the truth. What's this? Blood!'

In her sleep, she looked at her hands and cried, 'There's blood on my hands! He was an old man but he had a lot of blood in him.'

'Did you hear that?' said the doctor. 'What is she saying? It's terrible!'

Lady Macbeth went on talking. 'Macduff's wife, and their children! Where are they now? More blood! What are you looking at? There's no ghost. Look, Banquo's dead, I tell you. He can't come back from the dead. Go to bed. There's a knock at the door. Come, give me your hand. Go to bed.'

Then Lady Macbeth stopped talking and went back to her room.

candle it burns and gives light; in the past people used them to see at night

READING CHECK

1 Circle the correct words to complete the sentences about Macbeth's visit to the witches.

a He sees a (**soldier's**) **boy's** **baby's** head over the witches pot.

b The head cries: '**Macduff** **Malcolm** **a soldier** is going to hurt you.'

c He sees a **soldier** **king** **baby** with blood on its face and body.

d It says: 'Be happy, Macbeth! No **father's** **mother's** **parent's** son can hurt you!'

e He sees a young boy with a **dagger** **tree** **crown** in his hand.

f The boy says: 'When the trees begin to **talk** **walk** **die** , there's going to be trouble.'

2 Match the sentences with the people.

a Macbeth

b Lady Macbeth

c Macduff

d Banquo's ghost

e a messenger

1 [a] is angry with the witches.

2 [ ] has some terrible news for Macduff.

3 [ ] wants to kill Macbeth.

4 [ ] smiles at Macbeth.

5 [ ] doesn't like it when it's dark.

6 [ ] is one of Malcolm's friends.

7 [ ] laughs and says: 'Trees can't walk!'

8 [ ] cries: 'There's blood on my hands!'

WORD WORK

Use the words in the picture on page 31 to complete the sentences.

a What bad weather last night! Did you hear the rain and the .thunder. ?

b We can't stay here. This old building's going to fall down soon. It's not ....!

c That's the king over there: he's wearing a .... on his head.

d That angry man with the knife is coming nearer. He's going to .... me, I know.

e Macbeth's .... went to England, learned all about Macduff and Malcolm, and came and told him.

f Our son is only six months old. He's a ....

g It's dark in this hut. We can't read in the dark. We need a ....

baby attack crown
~~thunder~~
safe   candle   spy

GUESS WHAT

What happens in the next chapter? Tick the boxes.

		Yes	No
a	Macduff stays in England.	☐	☐
b	Macbeth kills many of Malcolm's soldiers in a battle.	☐	☐
c	Macduff dies.	☐	☐
d	Macbeth dies.	☐	☐
e	Malcolm is King of Scotland.	☐	☐
f	Lady Macbeth runs away.	☐	☐

Chapter 6 ❋ The trees begin to walk

The English army **marched** north to Scotland. Malcolm marched at the front of the army and his friend Macduff was next to him. Many Scottish soldiers **joined** the English army, because they **hated** Macbeth.

Not far from Macbeth's castle, there was a **forest**. 'Let's stop here,' said Malcolm. 'When we are ready, we can attack the castle. Soon, the people of Scotland are going to be happy again!'

❋

Macbeth stayed in his castle. Every day his spies brought him news.

'There is an army near the castle, my lord,' one of his spies told him.

'There are more than ten thousand soldiers!' said another. 'What are we going to do?'

'What's wrong? Are you afraid?' cried Macbeth angrily. 'This castle is **strong** and safe from attack.'

Macbeth wasn't worried about the English army. He thought about his visit to the witches' hut. He remembered the strange bloody baby and its words: *No mother's son can hurt you!*

But Macbeth wasn't happy. 'I have no friends,' he thought. 'I am the king, and everyone is afraid of me. But they hate me, too. My soldiers are leaving me, and they're joining Malcolm's army.'

Just then the doctor came to him from Lady Macbeth's room.

'How is my wife?' asked Macbeth.

'She needs to sleep, my lord. I want to help her, but I

march to walk into battle

join to go with

hate not to like

forest a place with lots of trees

strong not easy to attack

can't. She is worried about some strange things.' He was afraid to say more.

'I have no friends,' he thought.

'You must make her better, Doctor. But now I must get ready for battle,' said Macbeth.

Macbeth looked at the soldiers in front of him.

'Come on,' he shouted to them bravely. 'We must be ready. The English are going to attack us soon!'

Malcolm's army was now ready for battle.

'Listen, everyone,' said Malcolm. 'We're going to march towards Macbeth's castle soon. When we leave the forest, Macbeth is going to see us. When he sees us he can attack our army easily. So every man must **cut** a **branch** from a tree, and carry it in front of him. Then Macbeth can't see us.'

cut (*past* **cut**) to remove with a knife

branch part of a tree

33

All the soldiers cut big branches from the trees. Then the army began to march out of the forest to Macbeth's castle.

※

Macbeth's army wasn't very big, but he wasn't worried.

'Listen,' he said to his soldiers. 'There are thousands of English soldiers, I know, but they can't attack us because the castle is very strong. Soon, they're going to be hungry and tired. In the end, they're going to go home. We can wait!'

Suddenly Macbeth heard a noise. There was a lot of crying and worried voices in one of the rooms. A servant came out of the room. 'My lord, I have some terrible news. Your wife is dead.'

'My wife dead? Oh no! I wanted to make a wonderful future for the two of us,' said Macbeth, 'but now we have no future. Why did everything go wrong?'

Just then one of Macbeth's spies ran in. 'My lord, something very strange is happening. I looked at the forest a minute ago, and it began to move! The trees are coming nearer and nearer to the castle!'

'What!?' shouted Macbeth. 'No! Never! It isn't true!' He remembered his visit to the witches, and the young boy with the crown on his head. What did he say? *When the trees near your castle begin to walk, there is going to be trouble!*

'Trees can't walk, but the forest is moving! What's happening?' thought Macbeth. He was angry and worried now. 'What can I do? Is it better to stay here, or fight? I'm not safe here.'

Then he shouted to his soldiers: 'Open the doors! Quick! Meet the enemy! And – when you meet them – attack!'

※

Macbeth's soldiers ran out of the castle. When Malcolm saw them, he called to his army: 'Put your branches down. It's time to fight. This is going to be Macbeth's last day. Now, attack!'

The battle began. Many of Macbeth's soldiers didn't want to fight for Macbeth, and they joined Malcolm's army. But Macbeth fought bravely, and killed many of Malcolm's soldiers. 'My soldiers are leaving me,' he thought, 'but I am safe. Nobody can hurt me!'

Macduff was in the battle, too, but he didn't fight. He was only interested in one thing. 'I must find Macbeth,' he thought. 'He murdered my wife and children. I'm going to kill him!'

⁂

Soon, some of Malcolm's soldiers were near the castle.

'Let's go into the castle!' they cried. The castle doors were open, and some soldiers ran in. They were ready to fight, but Macbeth's soldiers were not in the castle.

Just then, Malcolm arrived. 'Come into the castle, my lord!' shouted his soldiers. He walked through the doors, tired but happy. 'Well done, my friends,' he told his soldiers. 'The battle is going to finish soon.'

⁂

The battle was bloody. Macbeth looked at all the dead soldiers in front of him.

'What shall I do?' thought Macbeth. 'I have no army now. My soldiers are running away. But I'm not going to die! I'm going to **fight**!'

Just then there was a loud, angry voice behind him. 'Macbeth!'

It was Macduff. Macbeth remembered the visit to the

fight (*past* **fought**) to hit someone again and again

sword a very long knife

witches, and the soldier's head: *Macduff is going to hurt you! Be careful!*

'Don't fight me, Macduff,' said Macbeth. 'Or I must kill you; and I don't want to kill you.'

'Don't speak to me, Macbeth. My **sword** is waiting to talk with you. Come on! Are you a man? Then fight!'

The two men fought angrily. Many times Macduff tried to stab Macbeth with his sword, but Macbeth was quick on his feet and strong.

In the end Macbeth laughed. 'Macduff, stop fighting and leave me,' he said. 'Know this! Nobody can kill me. A witch once told me that, and she knew all about the future. I remember her words well: *Be happy, Macbeth! No mother's son can hurt you!*'

'Are you a man? Then fight!'

'Perhaps your witch was right,' said Macduff, 'but I have news for you, Macbeth. My mother died an hour before I was born. The doctors cut me from her dead body. I didn't have a mother! Now, fight!'

Suddenly Macbeth felt ill. He couldn't fight. 'Why did I listen to the witches?' he thought. 'They once gave me **hope** for a wonderful future, but now I have nothing.'

'Come on, Macbeth,' called Macduff. 'What's wrong? Are you afraid?'

'I must be brave,' thought Macbeth. 'I must forget the witches. I can fight without their help!'

'Come on, Macduff,' cried Macbeth. 'I'm ready to fight, and I'm not going to stop. One of us is going to die today!'

Malcolm waited in the castle with his friends and soldiers. 'Did many people die in the battle?' he asked.

'Not many, my lord,' answered one of his soldiers. 'Most of Macbeth's soldiers didn't want to fight.'

But Malcolm was worried. 'Where is my friend Macduff?' he asked.

Just then, Macduff came into the castle. He was carrying something bloody in his hands. It was Macbeth's head!

'Scotland is safe again!' cried Macduff. 'Macbeth was never our king – he was a terrible murderer and he took the crown from Duncan. The true king of Scotland is here, in this castle,' he said. 'He is the son of Duncan. He is Malcolm, King of Scotland!'

Everyone cried happily: 'Malcolm, King of Scotland!'

hope good feelings about the future

READING CHECK

1 Correct the mistakes in these sentences.

                  north

a The English army marches ~~south~~ to Scotland.

b Malcolm and Macduff march at the back of the army.

c There are about twenty thousand soldiers in Malcolm's army.

d Macbeth isn't worried, because his army is strong.

e The doctor wants to kill Lady Macbeth.

f Macduff is angry and worried when the forest begins to move.

g Many of Macbeth's soldiers don't want to fight for Scotland.

h Macduff's mother died an hour after he was born.

2 Choose the best words to finish the sentences.

a Malcolm's army stops at . . .

1 ☐ a river.

2 ☐ a house.

3 ☑ a forest.

b Macbeth isn't happy, because . . .

1 ☐ he is very ill.

2 ☐ he has no friends.

3 ☐ he has lost all his money.

c When Malcolm's soldiers leave the forest, they are carrying . . .

1 ☐ guns and knives.

2 ☐ their hats and swords.

3 ☐ branches of trees.

d When Macbeth sees Macduff, he remembers . . .

1 ☐ his visit to the witches' hut.

2 ☐ his dead wife.

3 ☐ good old King Duncan.

WORD WORK

Complete the sentences with the pairs of words.

> ### *forest/march   swords/fight   hope/strong*
> ### *join/hate   branches/cut*

a Malcolm's soldiers ...... *cut* ...... *branches* ...... from the trees.

b Then the army begins to .... out of the ....

c Most of Macbeth's soldiers .... Malcolm's army because they
   .... Macbeth.

d Macbeth and Macduff .... with their ....

e Macbeth is .... , but Macduff kills him. Now there is ....
   for Scotland's future.

WHAT NEXT?

Here are some more famous people in stories by Shakespeare. Who would you like to read about? Why?

a Hamlet

One night, Hamlet sees the ghost of his dead father, the King of Denmark, in the castle. The ghost wants to talk to him . . .

b King Lear

The old king of England gives the country to his three daughters. But there is going to be trouble . . .

c Romeo and Juliet

They live in Verona, and are in love, but their families are enemies. Can they be happy?

PROJECT A Diaries

1 This is a page from Macbeth's diary. He wrote it the day after King Duncan's murder. Read it and answer the questions below.

Thursday

I did a terrible thing last night.

In the evening, I waited downstairs. My wife gave the king's servants a lot of wine before they went to bed. When my wife rang the bell, I went upstairs to the king's bedroom. His servants were in bed. They didn't wake up, because the wine was very strong. Their daggers were on the table next to their beds. I took the daggers and walked to the king's bed. And then I killed the king! Later I killed his servants, too. Everyone is going to think they are the murderers. But I'm worried about Banquo. Perhaps he knows the truth!

a Where did Macbeth wait in the evening?

b Who rang the bell?

c Where did Macbeth go?

d Where were Duncan's servants?

e Where were their daggers?

f Who did Macbeth kill first?

g Who did he kill later?

h Who is Macbeth worried about and why?

2 The same day, Lady Macbeth writes in her secret diary. Use the words below to complete her sentences.

Late last night, my husband went into

When he came back and spoke to me, I

because he had the servants' two daggers

He was afraid and didn't want to go back, so I

and went to the King's room. I left the daggers

and put blood on their hands and faces. I wasn't

Later, we washed our hands. Nobody is going to

My husband is going to be King, and I'm going to

We have a wonderful future. The three witches

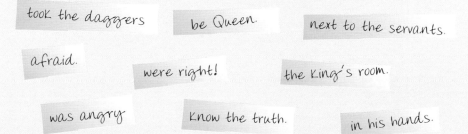

took the daggers

be Queen.

next to the servants.

afraid.

were right!

the King's room.

was angry

know the truth.

in his hands.

3 Write Macduff's diary for the same day. Use these words.

go	wake	friend	king	dead
murder	kill	servants	faint	

That morning I arrived at Macbeth's castle.

At the door I met

PROJECT B *Ghost Stories*

1 These pictures are about Martin Black and a thief. Match the sentences on page 43 with the pictures.

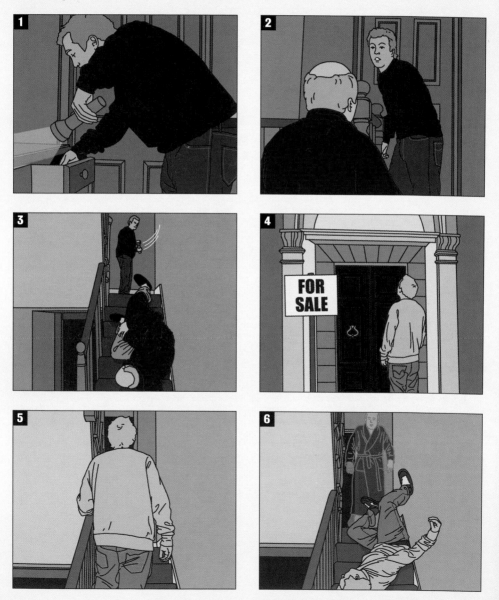

a ☐ The man killed Martin and ran away.

b ☐ When he saw Martin's ghost, he fell downstairs and died.

c ☐ One night a thief came into Martin Black's house and took all his money.

d ☐ Ten years later, the man bought a beautiful big house.

e ☐ The man heard a noise one evening and went upstairs.

f ☐ Martin heard a noise and got out of bed.

2 Write these sentences about Martin Black and the thief. Add *and* or *because* where necessary, and put the verbs in the past.

a The thief *come* into Martin's house / *take* all his money.

....

b Martin *get* out of bed / he *hear* a noise.

....

c The man *hit* Martin / *run* away with the money.

....

d Ten years later, the man *buy* a big house/ he *have* a lot of money.

....

e One evening, the man *hear* a noise / *go* upstairs.

....

f The man *want* to run away / he *be* afraid of Martin's ghost.

....

3   Look at the pictures below. Tell the story of Mary Smith and the young woman. Use
    these words and a dictionary to help you.

> *accident   to help   hospital   a bend in the road*
> *to wave   stormy   to lie   to save (her) life*

1 1995

2

3

4 2005

5

6

....
....
....
....
....
....
....
....
....
....
....